1 PIANO, 4 HANDS

PIANO DUET PLAY·ALONG VOLUME 19

PIRATES OF THE CARIBBEAN

ARRANGED BY CAROL KLOSE

To access audio, visit:
www.halleonard.com/mylibrary

3409-1877-2151-7132

ISBN 978-1-4234-3643-0

Walt Disney Music Company
Wonderland Music Company, Inc.

DISTRIBUTED BY

7777 W. BLUEMOUND RD. P.O. BOX 13819 MILWAUKEE, WI 53213

In Australia Contact:
Hal Leonard Australia Pty. Ltd.
4 Lentara Court
Cheltenham, Victoria, 3192 Australia
Email: ausadmin@halleonard.com.au

Visit Hal Leonard Online at
www.halleonard.com

CONTENTS

THE BLACK PEARL

from Walt Disney Pictures' PIRATES OF THE CARIBBEAN: THE CURSE OF THE BLACK PEARL

SECONDO

Music by
KLAUS BADELT

THE BLACK PEARL

from Walt Disney Pictures' PIRATES OF THE CARIBBEAN: THE CURSE OF THE BLACK PEARL

PRIMO

Music by
KLAUS BADELT

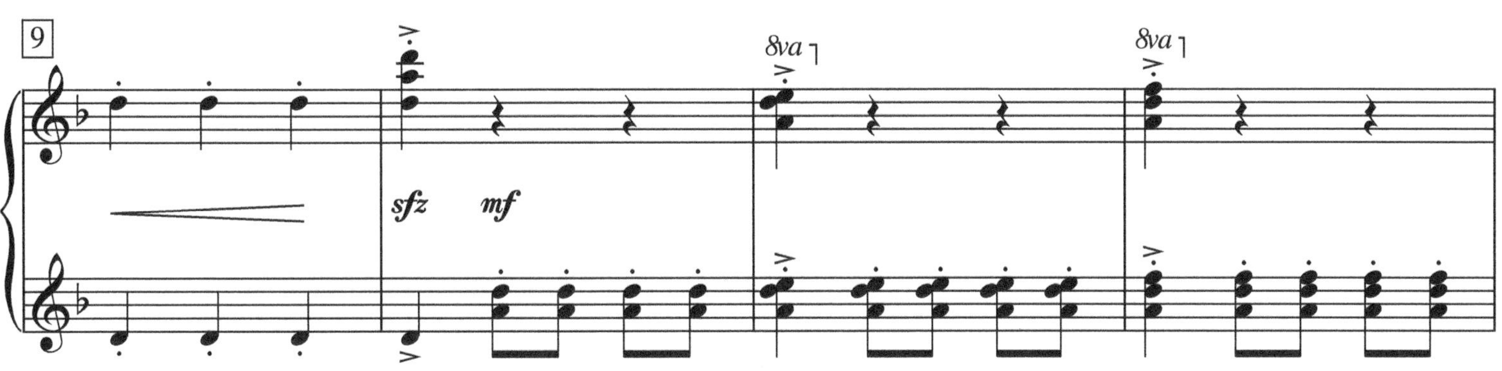

17

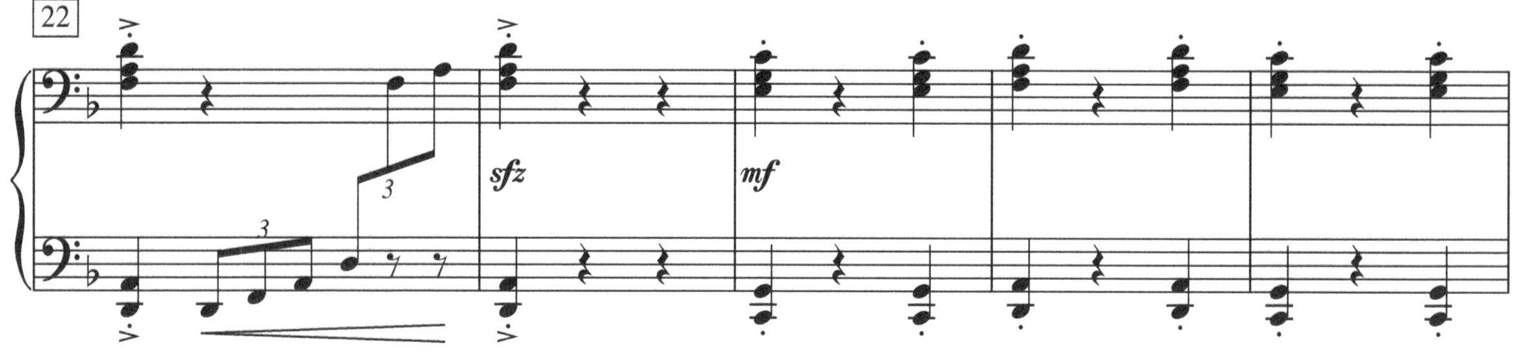
22
3
3
sfz
mf

27

32

36

17
22
sfz
f
27
8va
mf
32
36
3
3

40
f
45
sfz
f
49
53
ff
57
p mysteriously
8vb

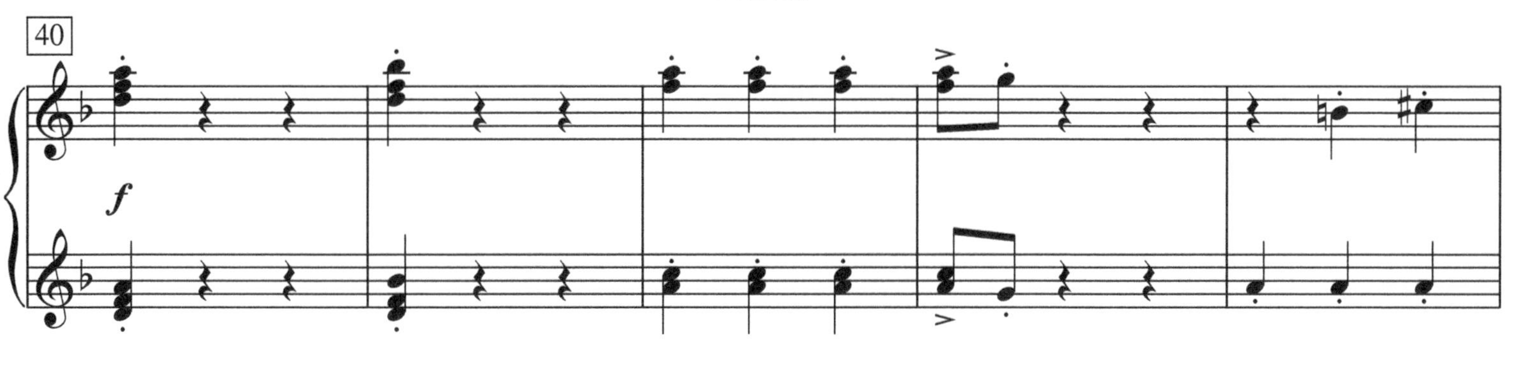
40
f

45
8va
sfz
f

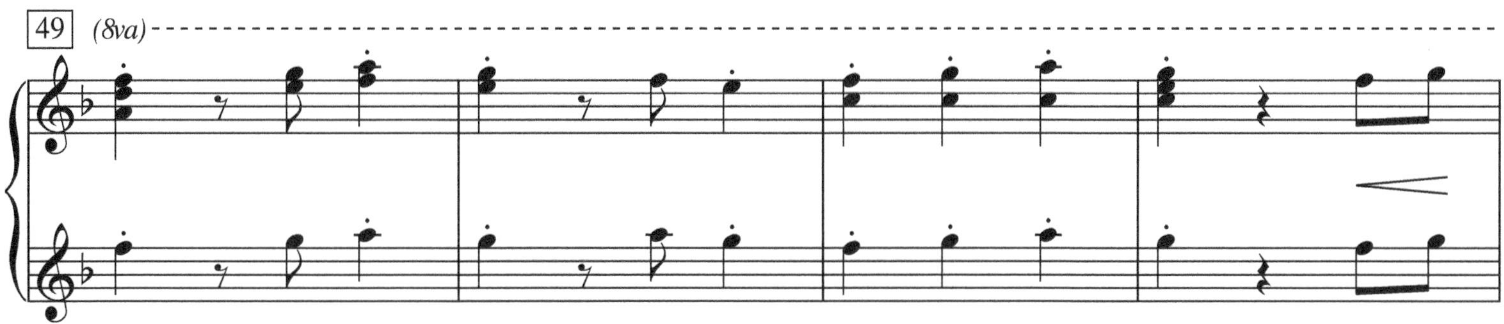
49
(8va)

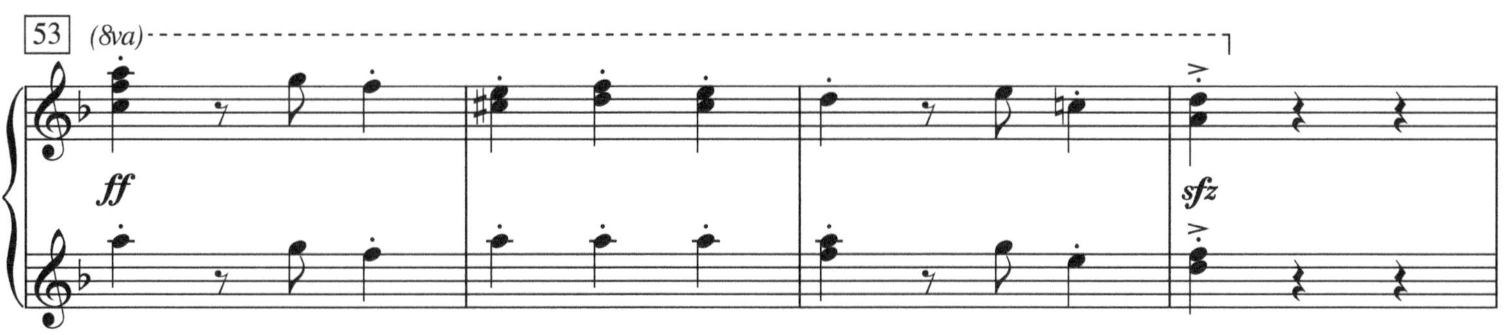
53
(8va)
ff
sfz

57
p mysteriously

62
(8vb)

67
(8vb)

72
8vb to end

78
pp dim. to end

83
ppp

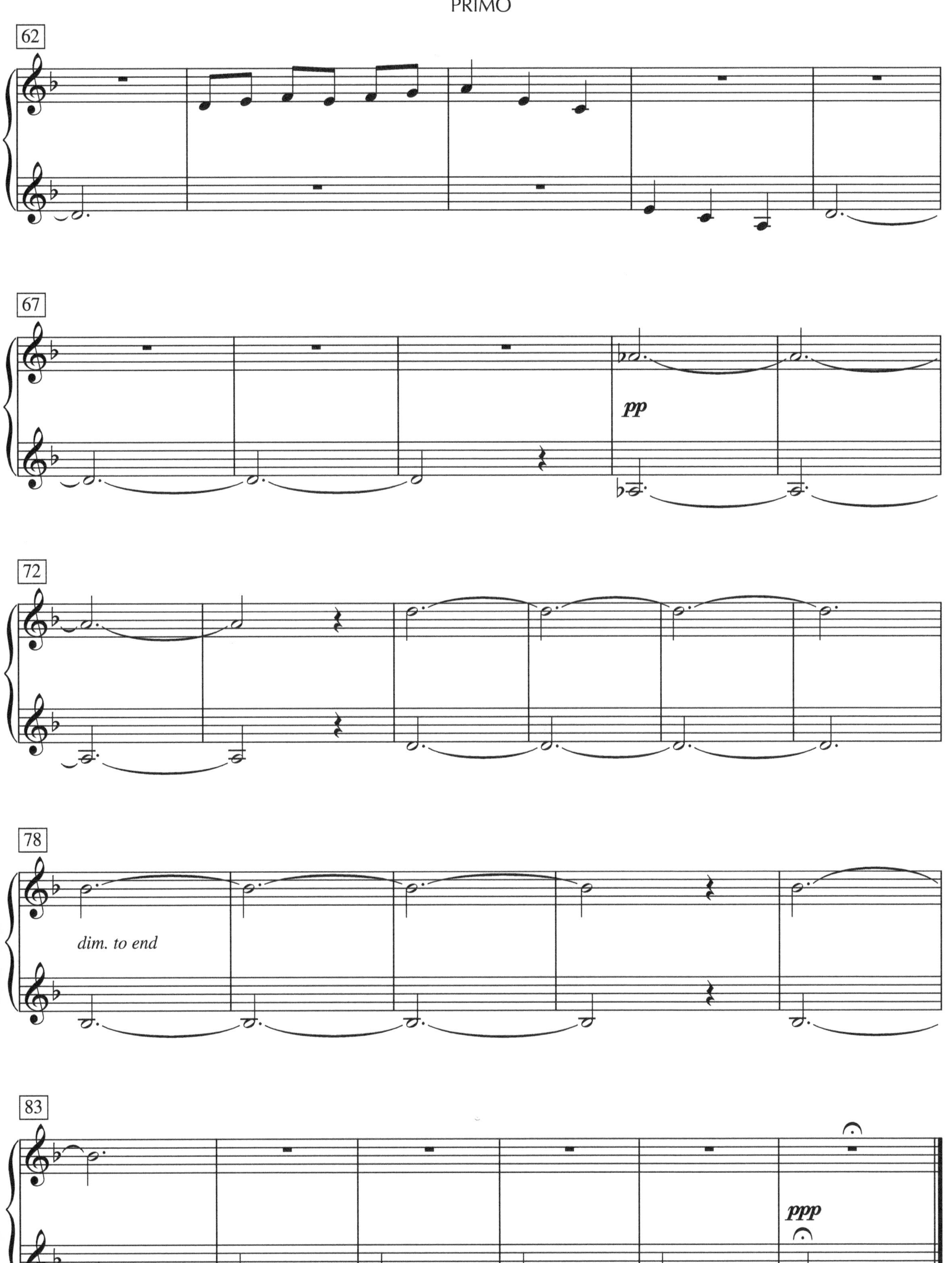
62
67
pp
72
78
dim. to end
83
ppp

BRETHREN COURT

from Walt Disney Pictures' PIRATES OF THE CARIBBEAN: AT WORLD'S END

SECONDO

Music by
HANS ZIMMER

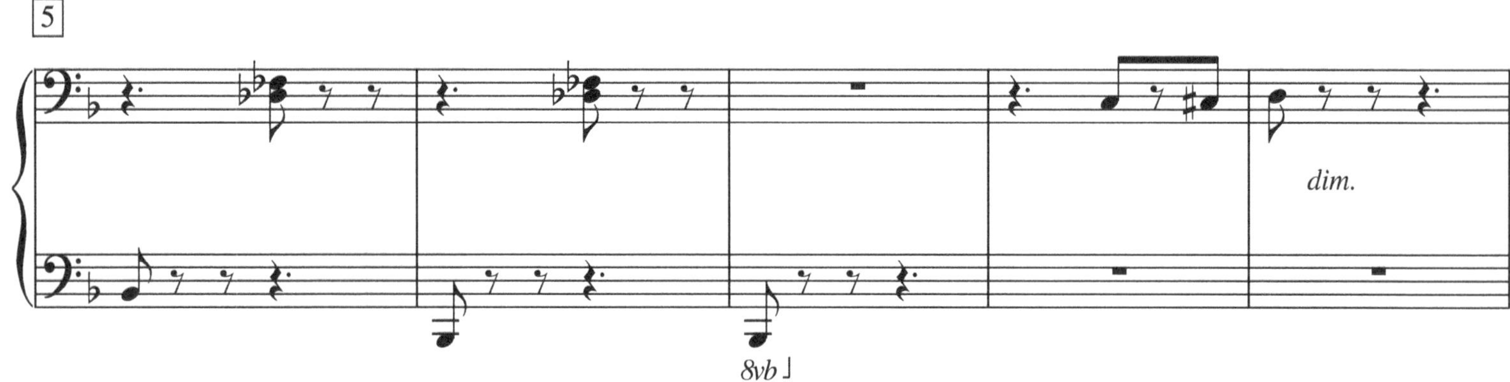

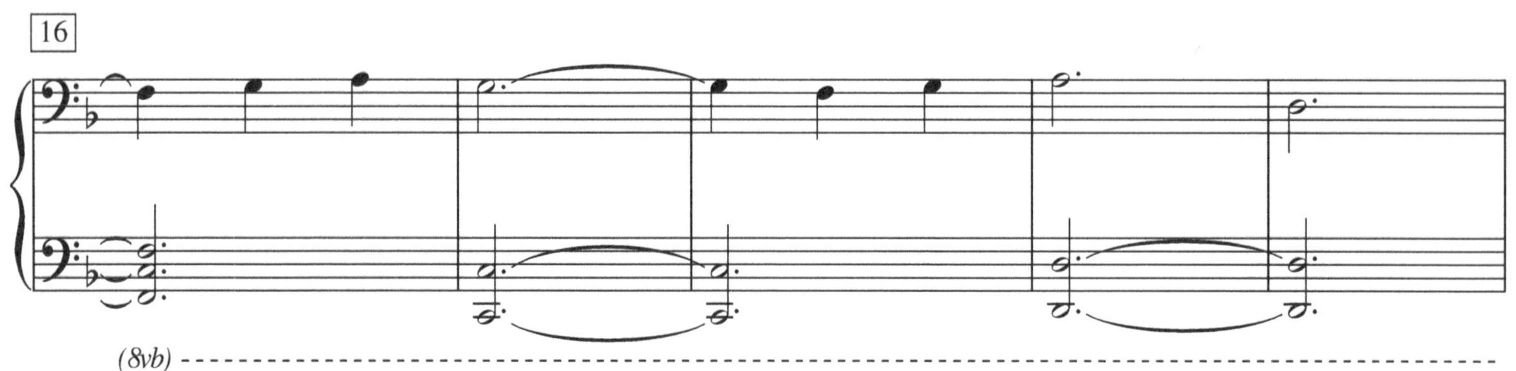

BRETHREN COURT

from Walt Disney Pictures' PIRATES OF THE CARIBBEAN: AT WORLD'S END

PRIMO

Music by
HANS ZIMMER

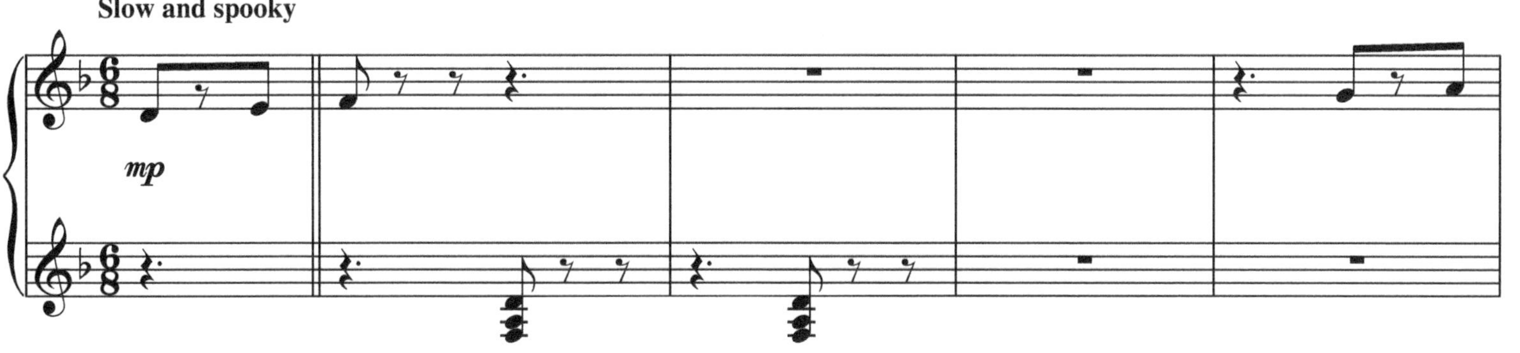

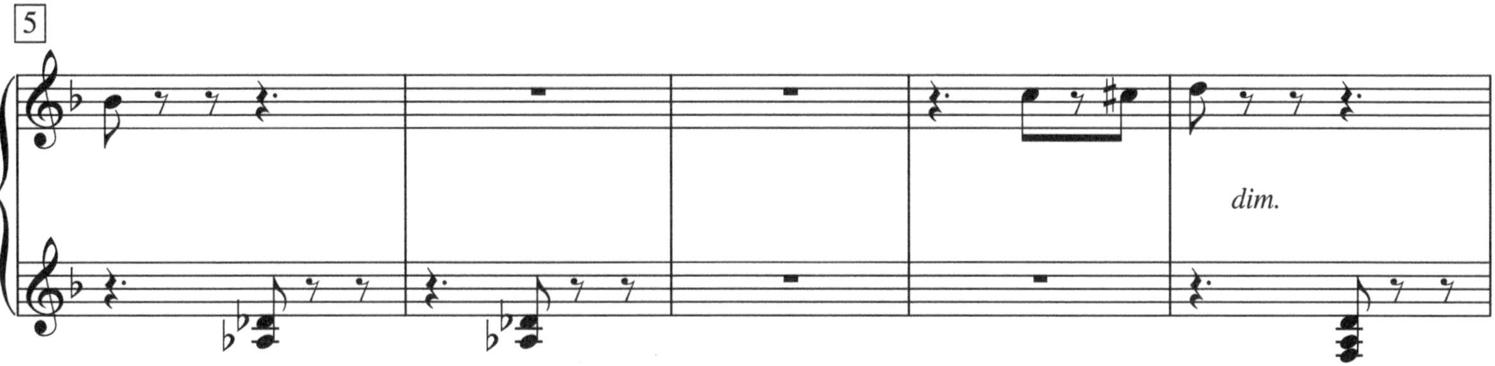

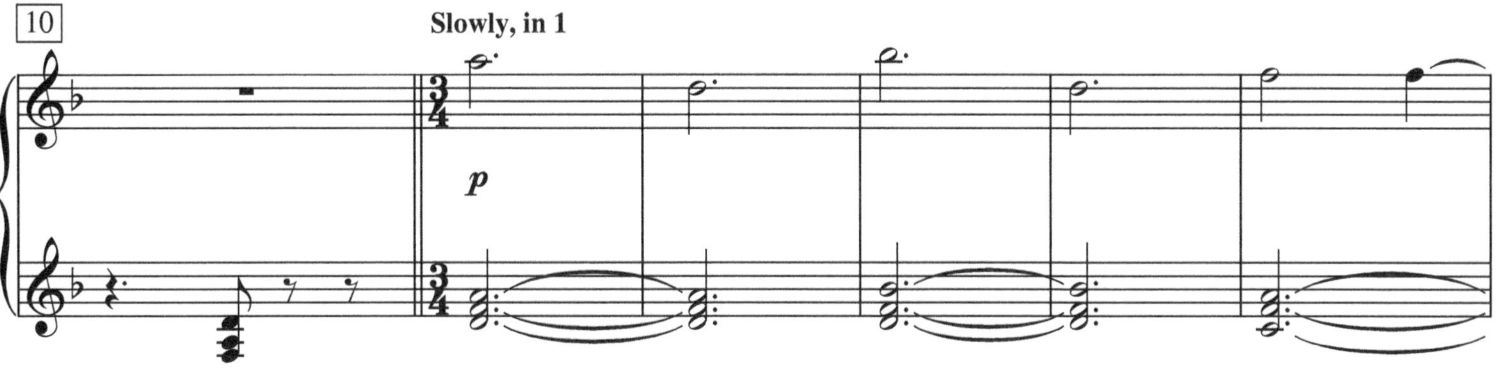

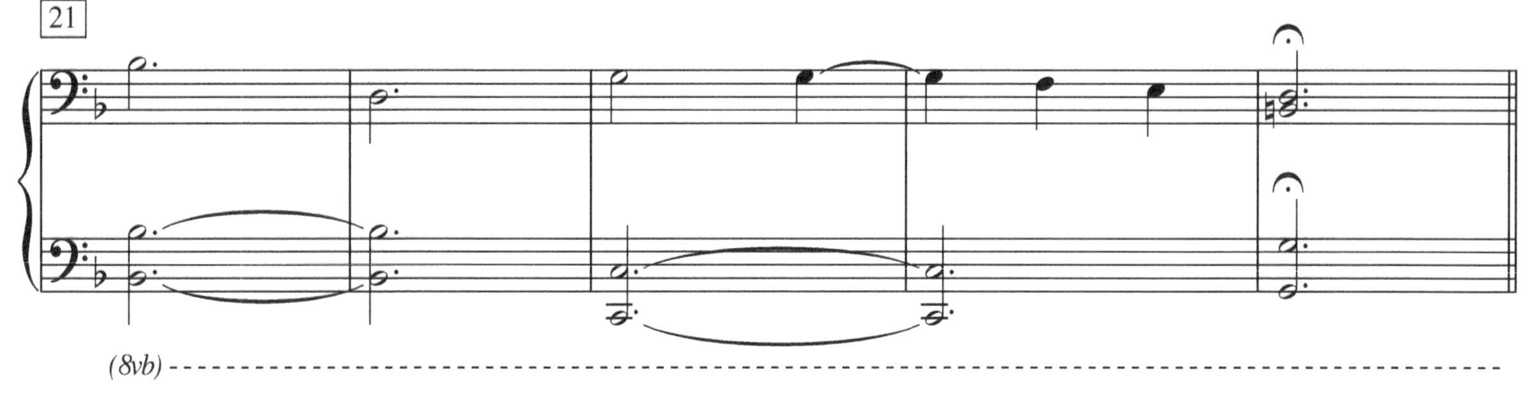
21
(8vb)

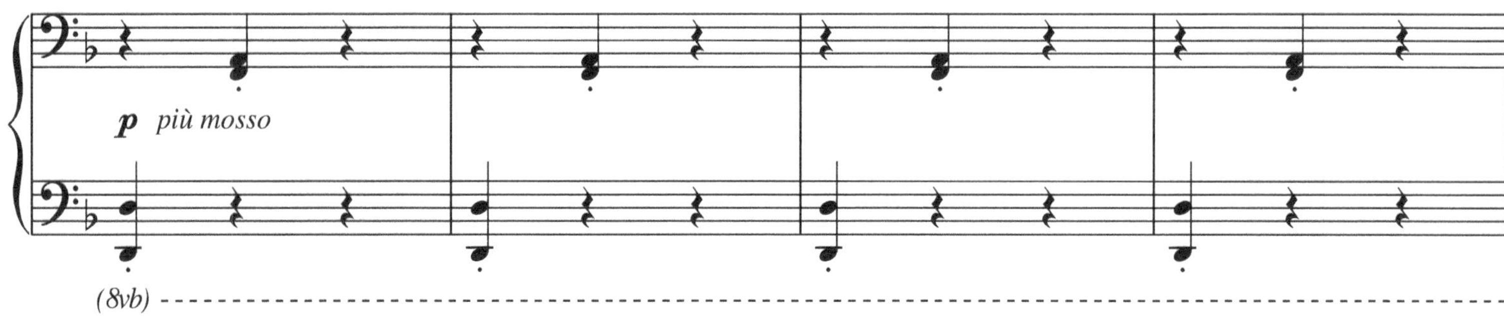
26
Moderately
p più mosso
(8vb)

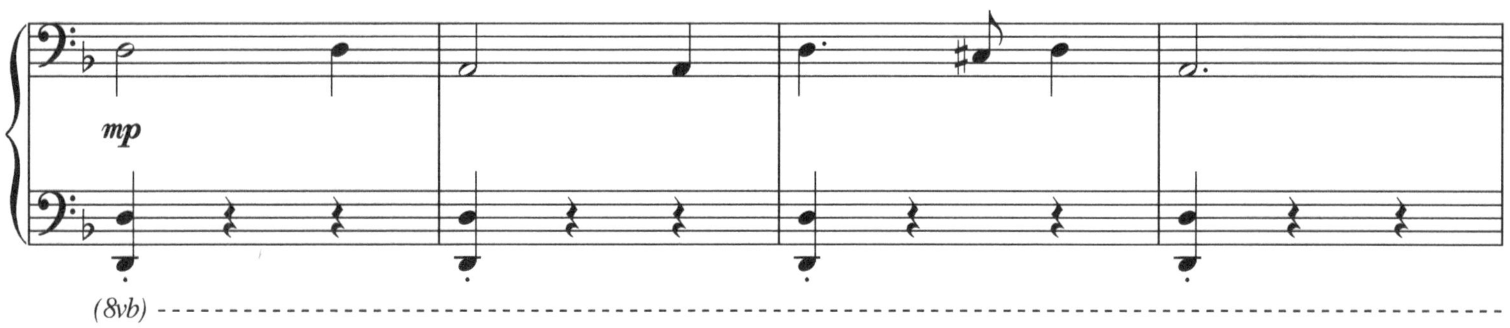
30
mp
(8vb)

34
(8vb)

38

21
26
Moderately
p più mosso
30
mp
34
38

42
46
1
2
3
1
4
5
1
mp
staccato simile
50
54
p
58
pp

42
46
mf
50
54
mp
58
p

HE'S A PIRATE

from Walt Disney Pictures' PIRATES OF THE CARIBBEAN: THE CURSE OF THE BLACK PEARL

SECONDO

Music by
KLAUS BADELT

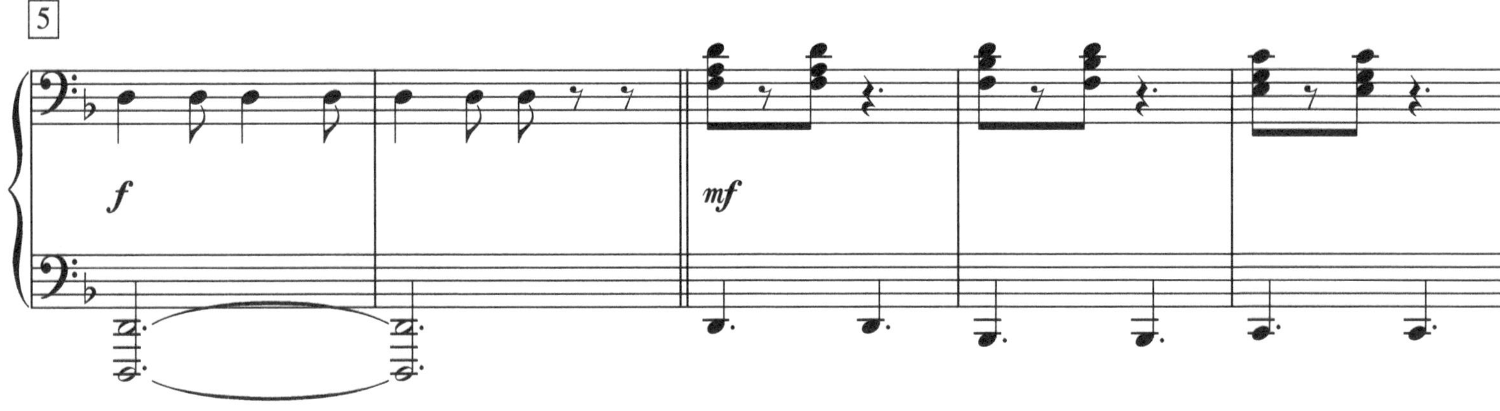

HE'S A PIRATE

from Walt Disney Pictures' **PIRATES OF THE CARIBBEAN: THE CURSE OF THE BLACK PEARL**

PRIMO

Music by
KLAUS BADELT

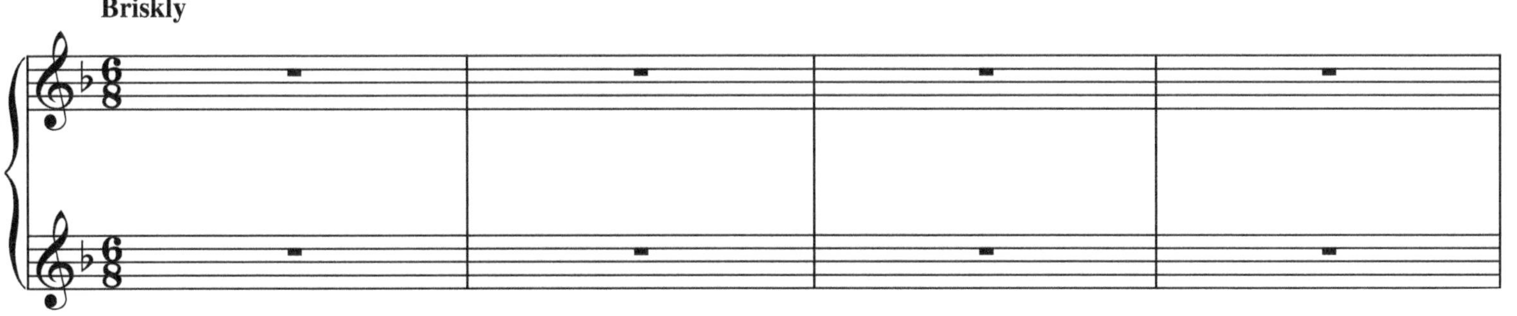

20
25
30
35
(♪ = ♪)
39
cresc.
sfz
sfz

20
25
30
8va
35
(8va)
(♪ = ♪)
39
(8va)
cresc.
sfz
sfz

43
f
48
53
p
58
mp
63

43
(8va)
f
f
48
53
mp
58
mf
63

68
mf
73
78
83
p sub.
8vb
88
(8vb)
pp

68
f
73
78
83
88
pp

JACK SPARROW

from Walt Disney Pictures' PIRATES OF THE CARIBBEAN: DEAD MAN'S CHEST

SECONDO

Music by
HANS ZIMMER

Moderately slow, comically

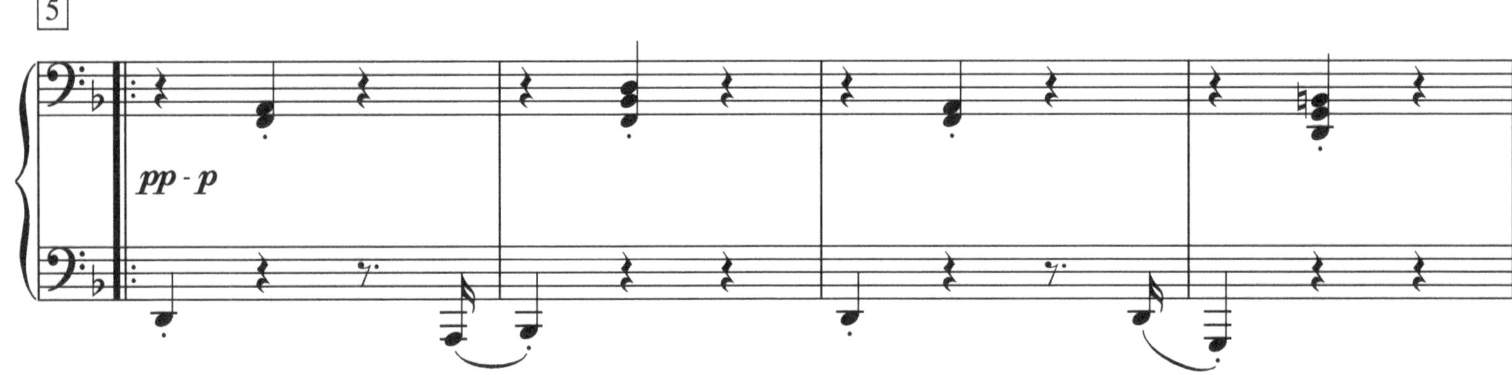

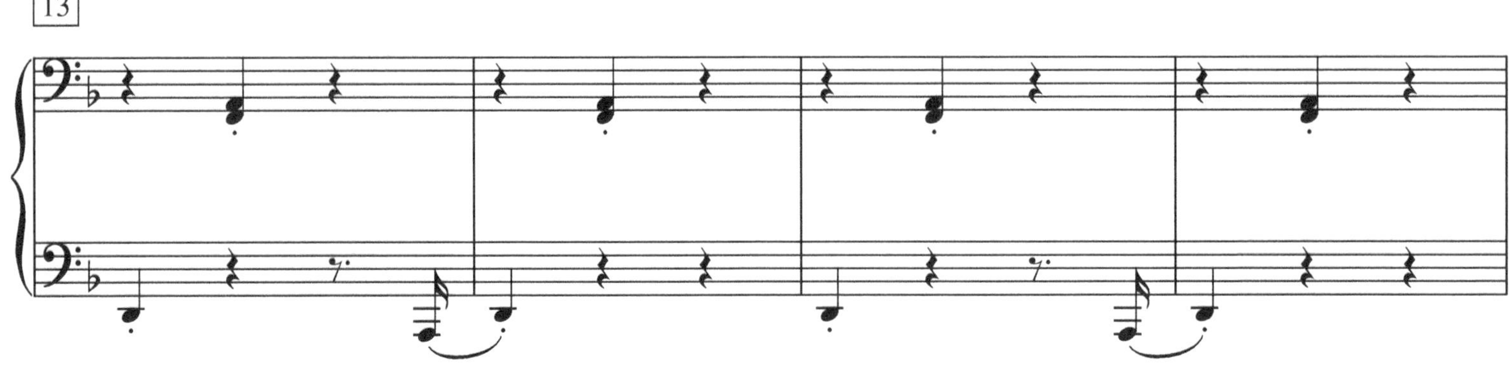

JACK SPARROW

from Walt Disney Pictures' PIRATES OF THE CARIBBEAN: DEAD MAN'S CHEST

PRIMO

Music by
HANS ZIMMER

Moderately slow, comically

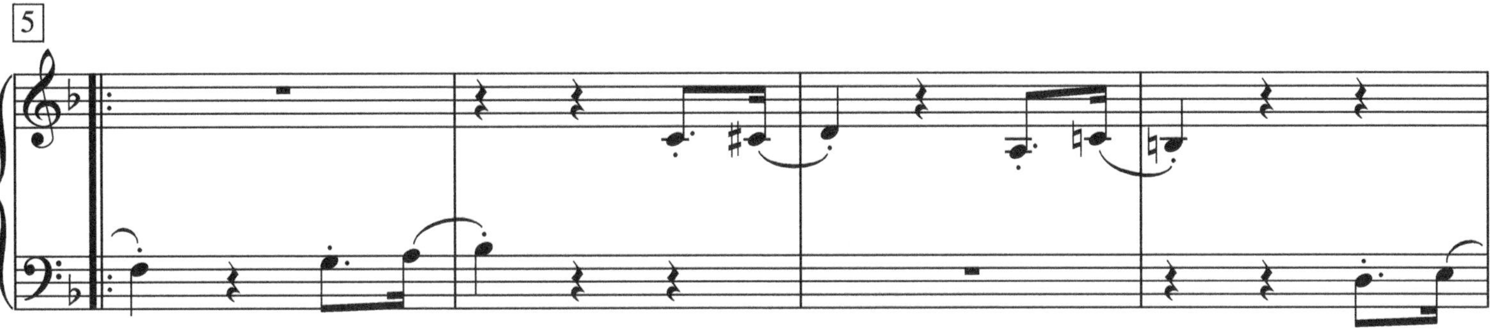

17
p
21
1.
2.
Slightly faster
f
26
p
31
Lively
più mosso
p
non legato
36

17
p
3
21
1.
2.
Slightly faster
mp
f
26
p
31
Lively
più mosso
p
36

41
mp

46

51
mp

56
f
ff
mp

61
cresc.

41
mp
non legato

46

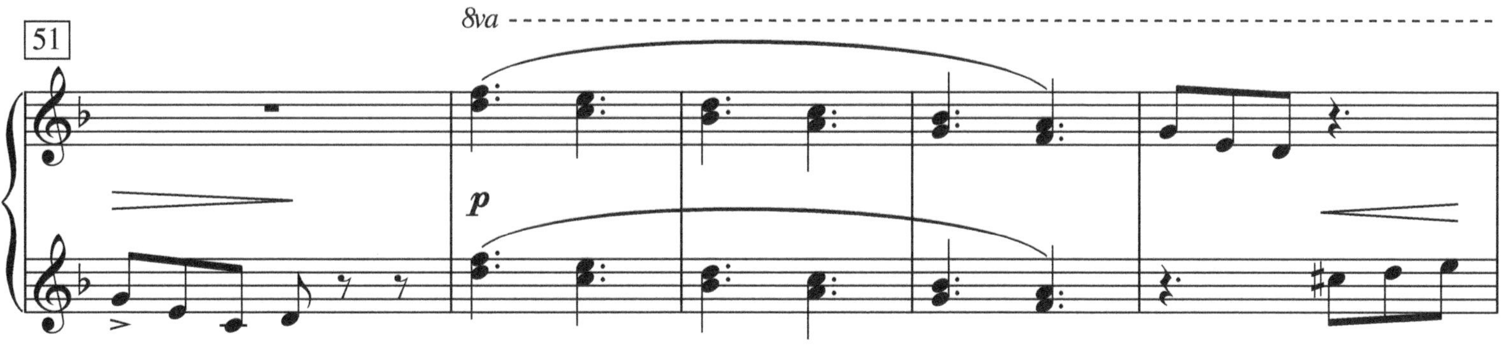
51
8va
p

56
(8va)
f
ff
mf

61
cresc.

66
mp

70
f

74
mf

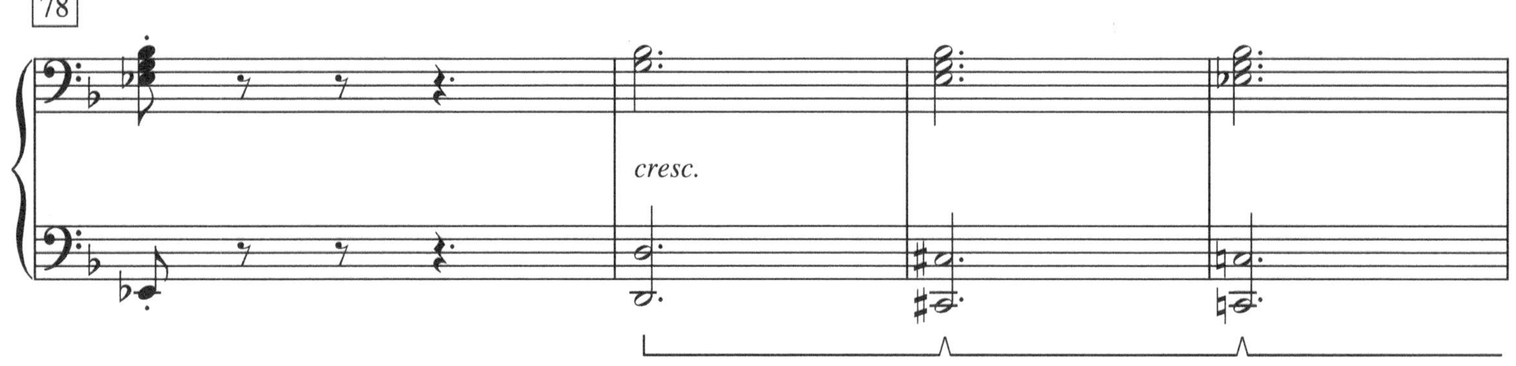
78
cresc.

82
mp

66
mf
70
f
74
mf
78
cresc.
82
mp

86
ff
90
1.
94
2.
98
102

86
f
90
1.
94
2.
98
102

106

110
p

115
To Coda

119

123

106

110

sfz

115

To Coda

119

123

127
D.S. al Coda
mp

CODA
f

135

140
ff

144
sfz

127
D.S. al Coda
CODA
ff
135
140
144
8va
sfz

THE KRAKEN

from Walt Disney Pictures' PIRATES OF THE CARIBBEAN: DEAD MAN'S CHEST

SECONDO

Music by
HANS ZIMMER

Moderately

THE KRAKEN

from Walt Disney Pictures' PIRATES OF THE CARIBBEAN: DEAD MAN'S CHEST

PRIMO

Music by
HANS ZIMMER

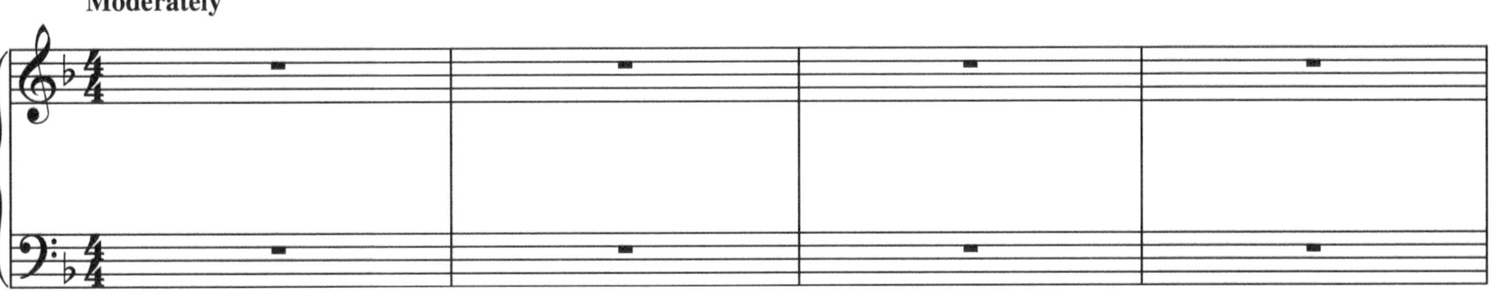

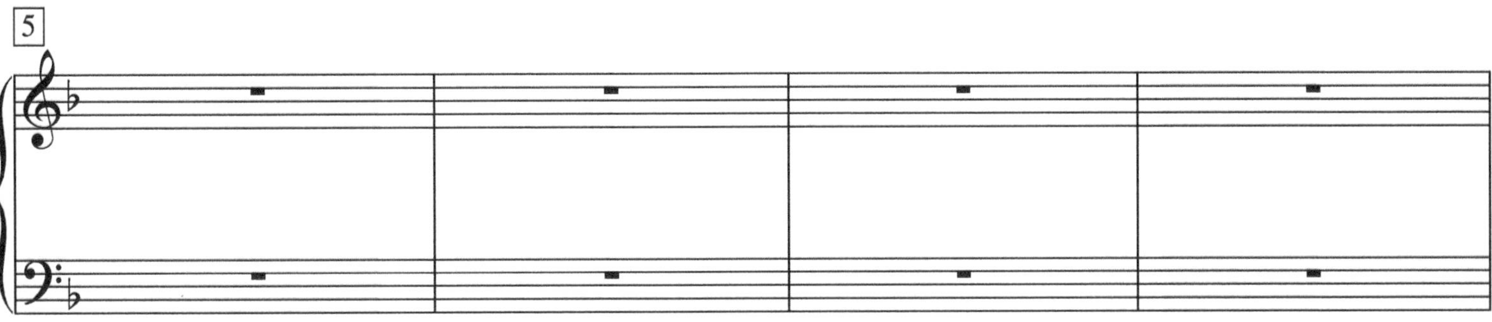

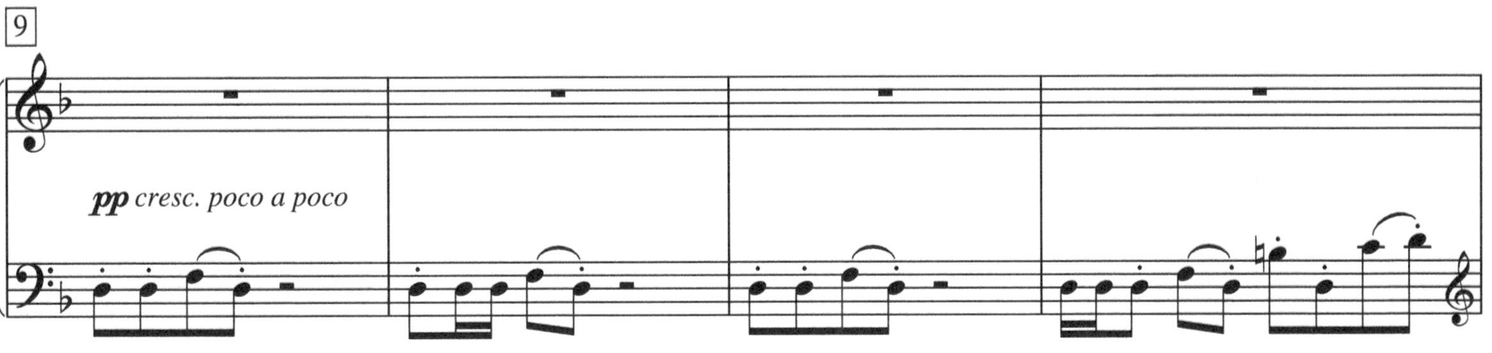

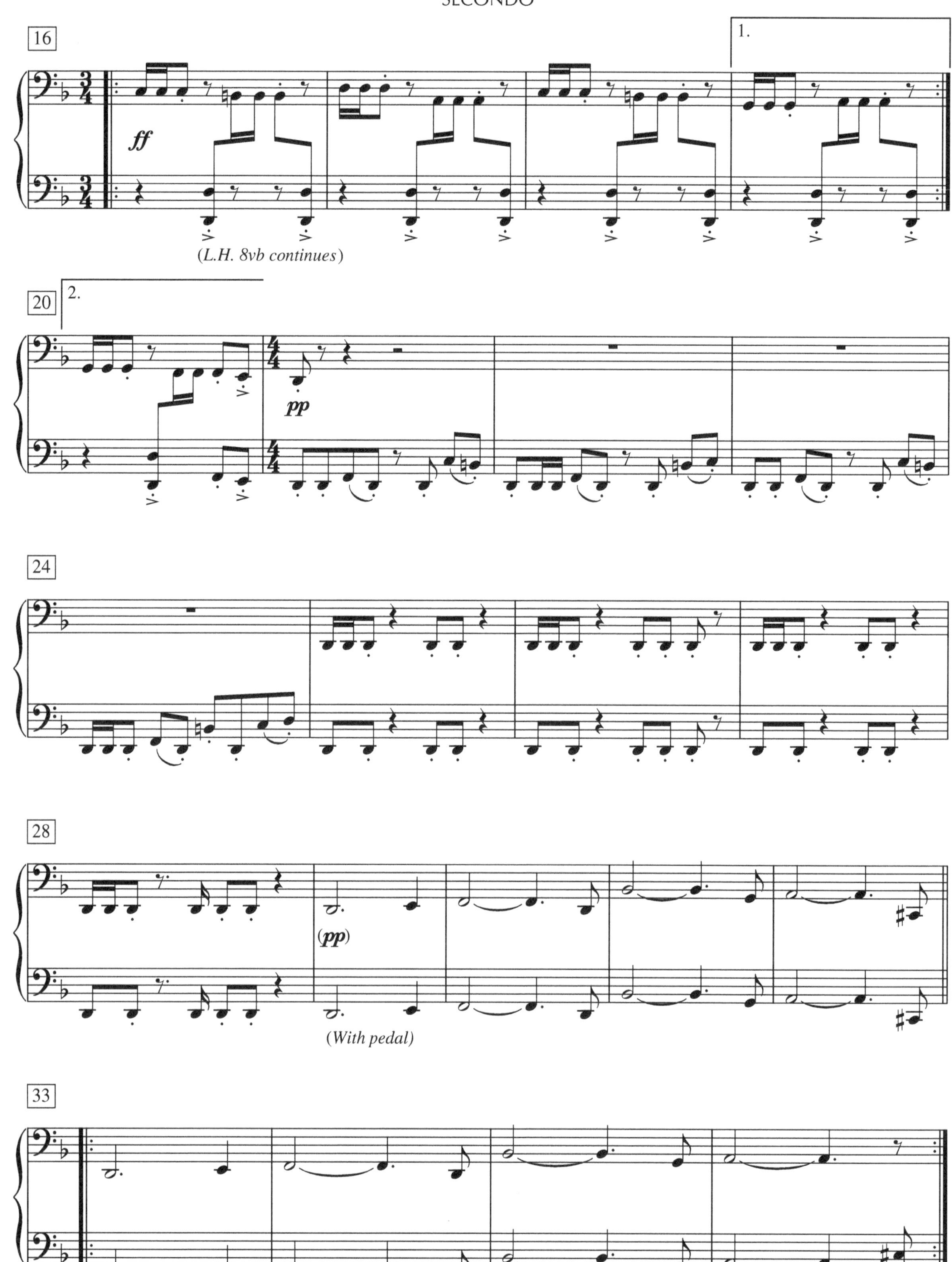
16
1.
ff
(L.H. 8vb continues)
20
2.
pp
24
28
(pp)
(With pedal)
33

16
1.
ff

20
2.
pp

24
pp

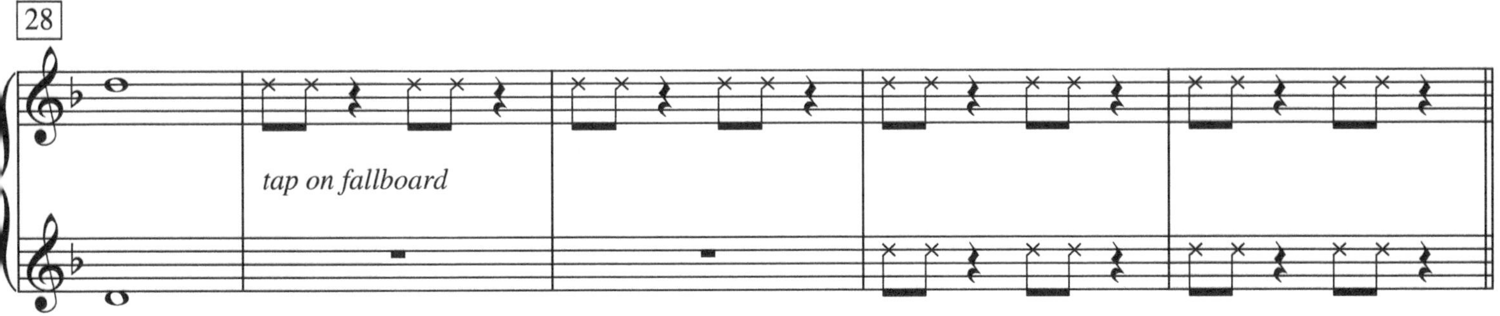
28
tap on fallboard

33
mp à la pipe organ

37
ff subito
(L.H. 8vb continues)
40
pp sub.
no pedal
44
p
48
ff sub.
51
1.
2.
sfz

37
8va R.H.
ff subito
40
(8va)
44
p
48
ff sub.
51
1.
2.
sfz

THE MEDALLION CALLS

from Walt Disney Pictures' PIRATES OF THE CARIBBEAN: THE CURSE OF THE BLACK PEARL

SECONDO

Music by
KLAUS BADELT

THE MEDALLION CALLS

from Walt Disney Pictures' **PIRATES OF THE CARIBBEAN: THE CURSE OF THE BLACK PEARL**

PRIMO

Music by
KLAUS BADELT

13
mf
16
19
pp
p
8vb
23
p
8vb
27
mp

13
f
16
19
mp
pp chime-like
23
mp
27
mf

31
34
37
mf
40
p sub.
8vb
44
(8vb)
pp

31
34
37
f
40
44
(tap on fallboard)

ONE DAY

from Walt Disney Pictures' PIRATES OF THE CARIBBEAN: AT WORLD'S END

SECONDO

Music by
HANS ZIMMER

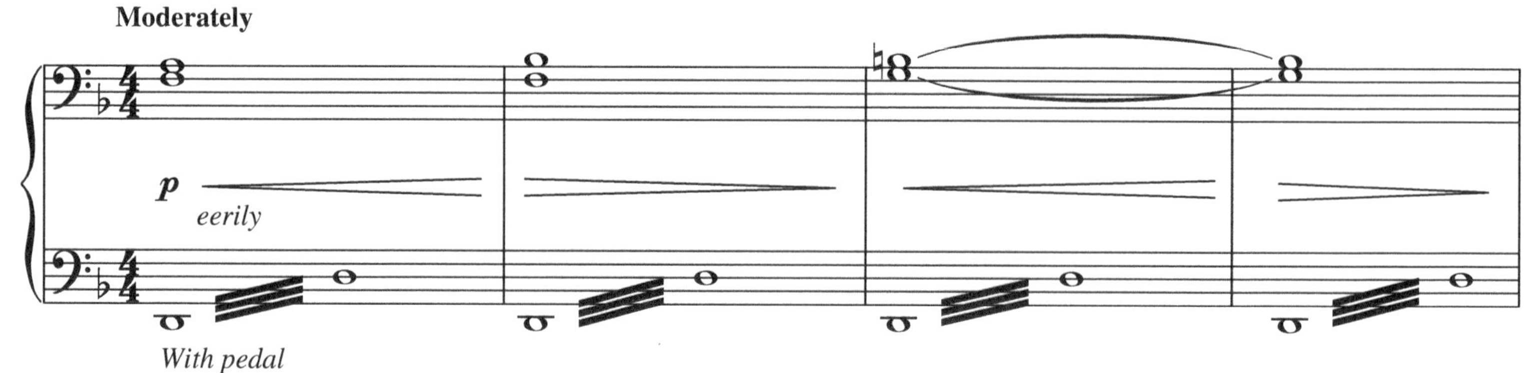

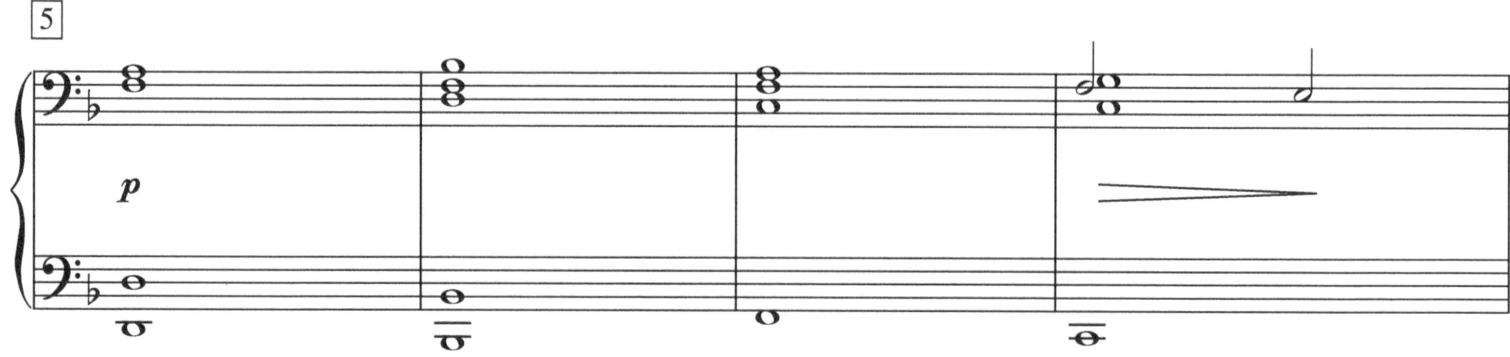

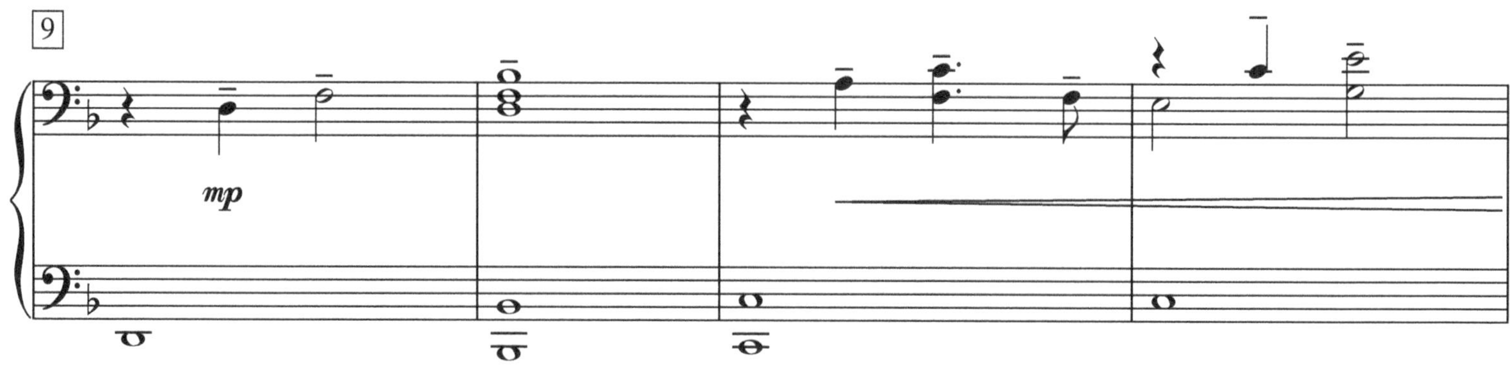

ONE DAY

from Walt Disney Pictures' PIRATES OF THE CARIBBEAN: AT WORLD'S END

PRIMO

Music by
HANS ZIMMER

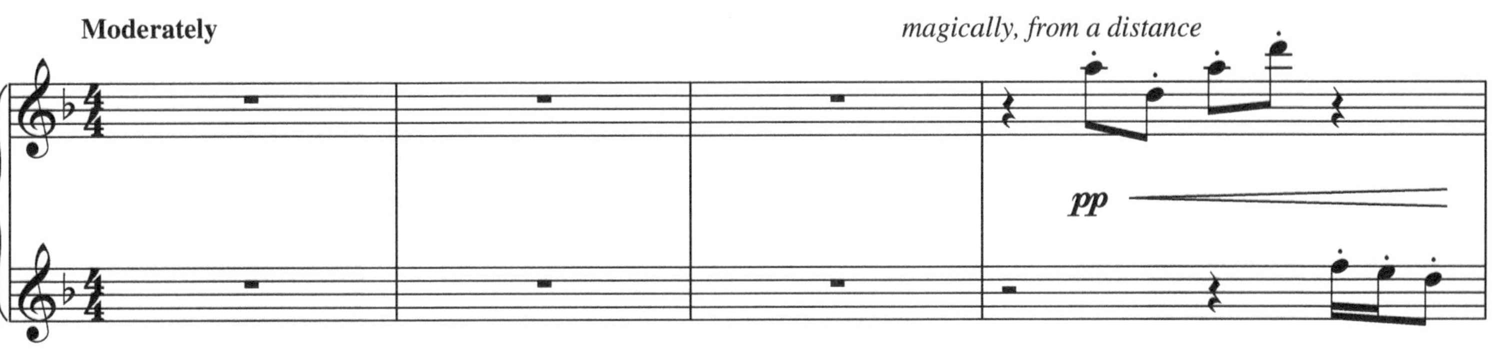

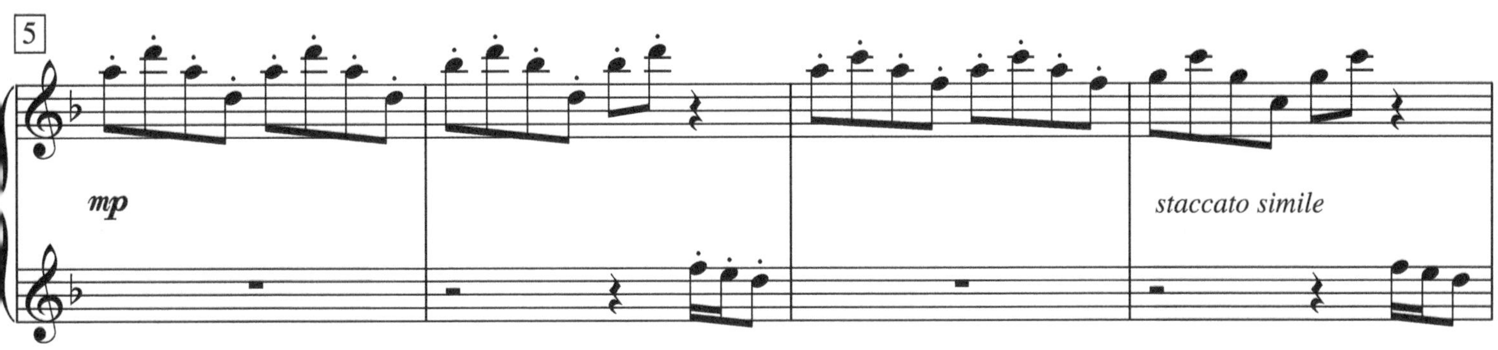

17
21
f
8vb
25
p
(8vb)
29
ff
(8vb)
32
Slower, but with motion
pp
(8vb)

(8va)
17
3
3
(8va)
21
ff
(8va)
25
mp
29
ff
32
Slower, but with motion
ppp
mp

35
simile
(8vb)
38
(8vb)
41
mp
(8vb)
44
(8vb)
47
(8vb)

35
38
p warmly
41
mf
44
47

49
mf
(8vb)
52
1.
2.
legato
mp
(8vb)
loco
55
8vb
58
8vb
62
f
p
rit.
pp
8vb

49
mp
52
1.
2.
mf legato
55
58
62
3
f
p
rit.
pp

UP IS DOWN

from Walt Disney Pictures' PIRATES OF THE CARIBBEAN: AT WORLD'S END

SECONDO

Music by
HANS ZIMMER

UP IS DOWN

from Walt Disney Pictures' **PIRATES OF THE CARIBBEAN: AT WORLD'S END**

PRIMO

Music by
HANS ZIMMER

20
mp
24
1.
28
2.
mf
32
36

20
mf
24
1.
28
2.
mp
32
8va
36
tr

39
f
43
1.
2.
48
mf
sfz
8vb
52
sfz
8vb
sfz
8vb
56
mf

39
f
43
1.
2.
48
mf
52
56
mp

61
66
71
f
76
81
molto rit.
sfz

61
66
71
f
76
81
molto rit.
sfz

WHEEL OF FORTUNE

from Walt Disney Pictures' PIRATES OF THE CARIBBEAN: DEAD MAN'S CHEST

SECONDO

Music by
HANS ZIMMER

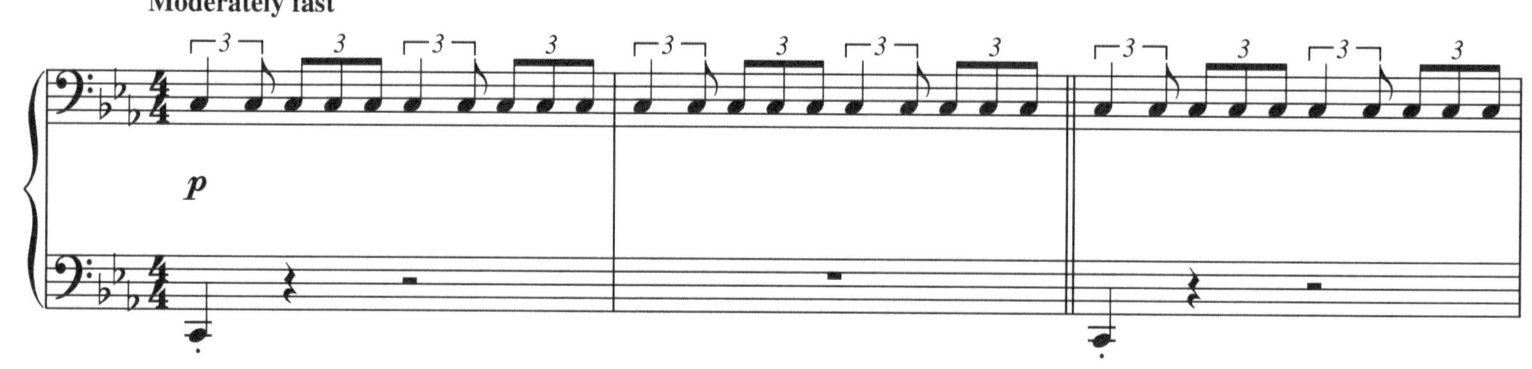

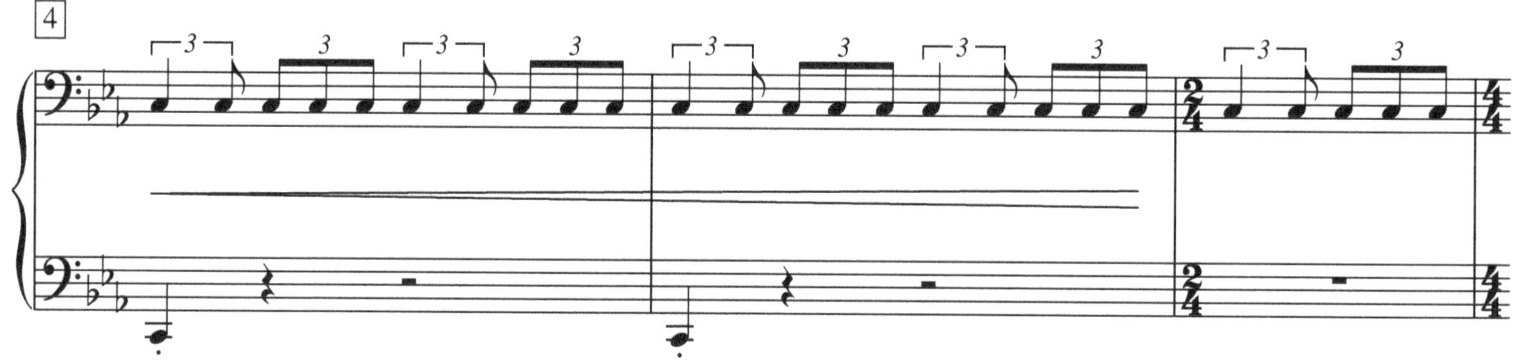

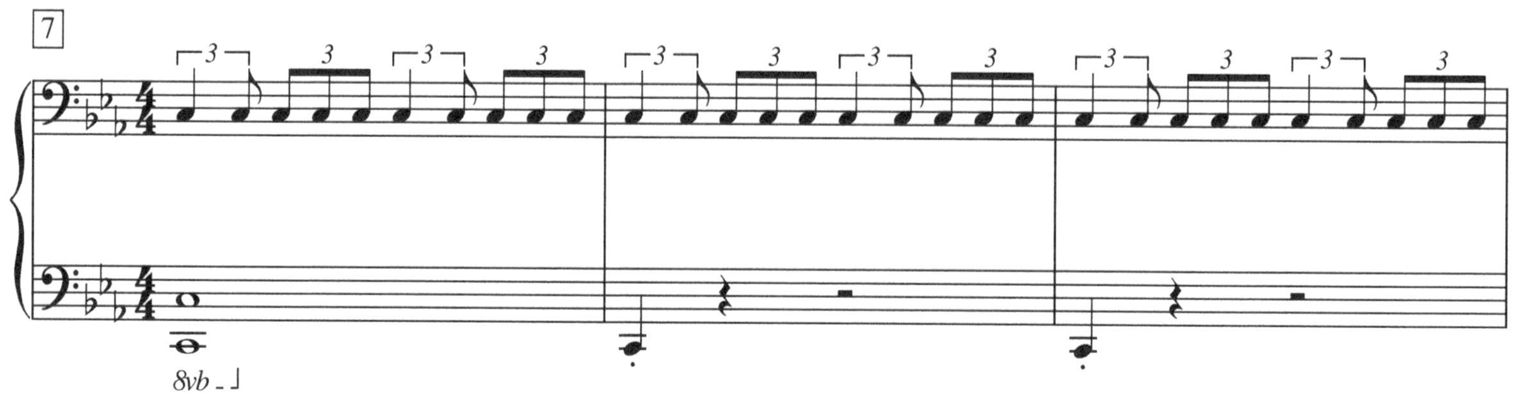

WHEEL OF FORTUNE

from Walt Disney Pictures' PIRATES OF THE CARIBBEAN: DEAD MAN'S CHEST

PRIMO

Music by
HANS ZIMMER

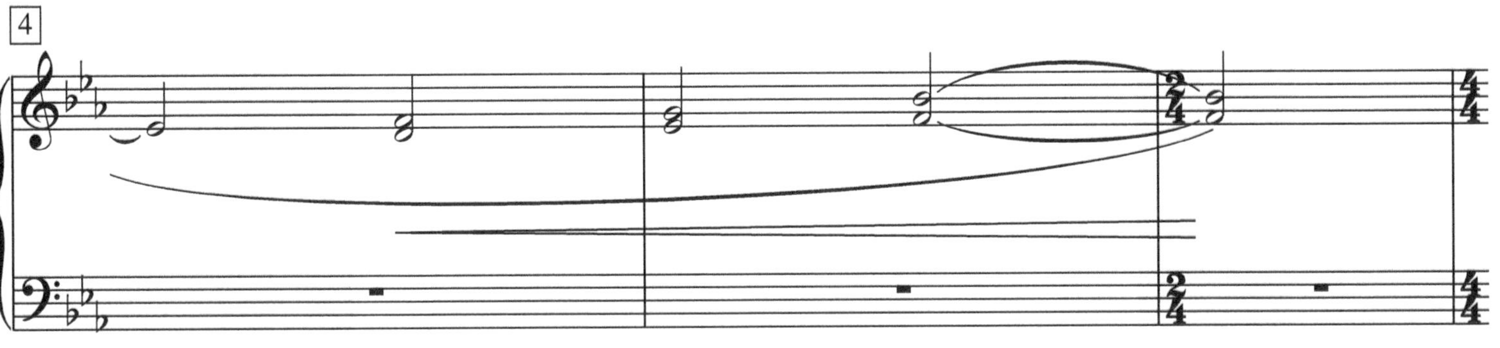

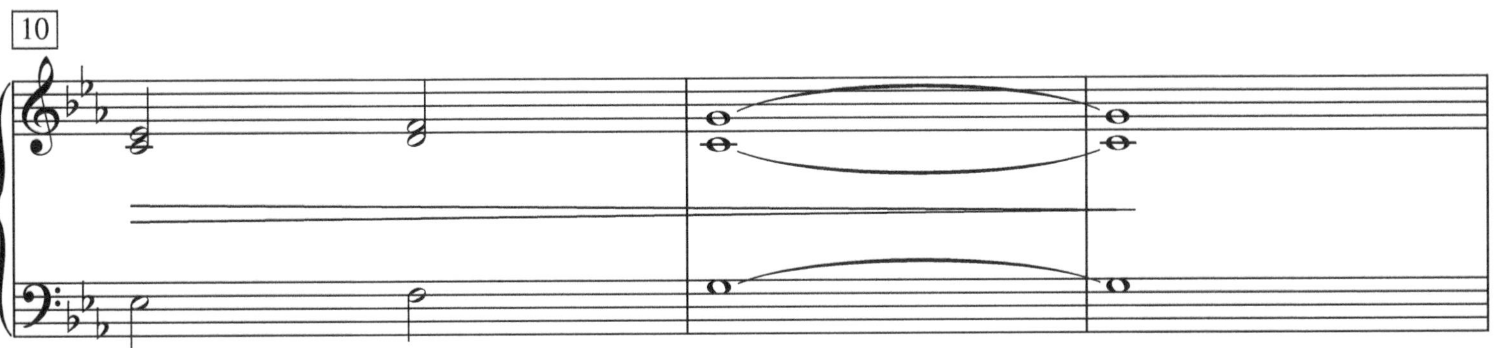

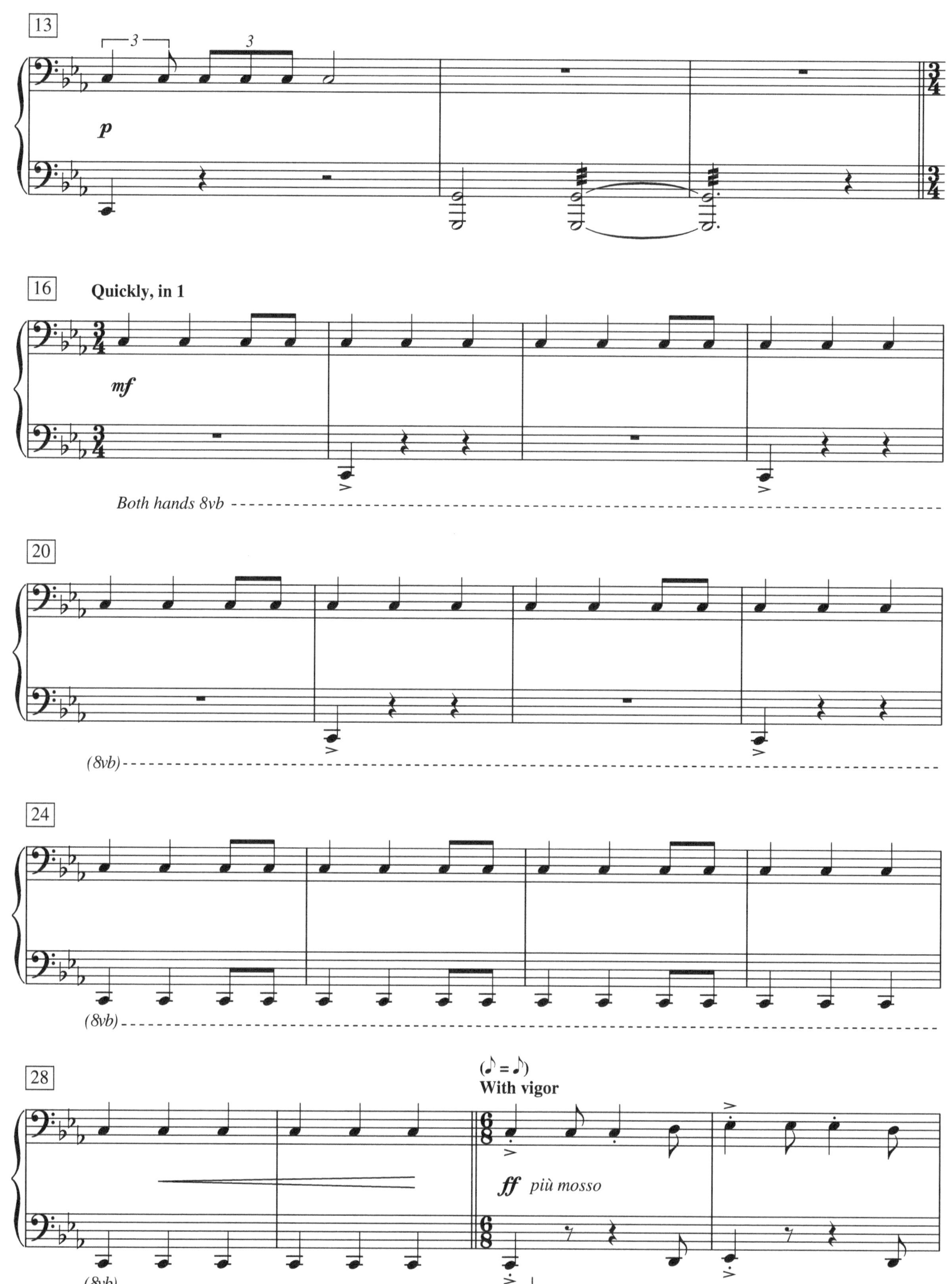
13
p
16
Quickly, in 1
mf
Both hands 8vb
20
(8vb)
24
(8vb)
28
(♪ = ♪)
With vigor
ff più mosso
(8vb)

13
f
16
Quickly, in 1
20
24
28
(♪ = ♪)
With vigor
ff più mosso

32
36
mp with a sense of urgency
40
fff
sfz
44
sfz
sfz
ff
48

32
36
1
mp with a sense of urgency
3
40
2
1
3
fff
1
2
3
44
ff
48

53
f
56
59
1.
2.
8vb
8vb
62
f
65

53
f
56
59
1.
2.
62
ff
65

68
mp
72
ff
8vb
76
80
84
sfz

68
mp
72
ff
76
80
84
8va
sfz
p subito

88
pp
92
f
8vb
96
p
100
cresc. poco a poco
104
fff

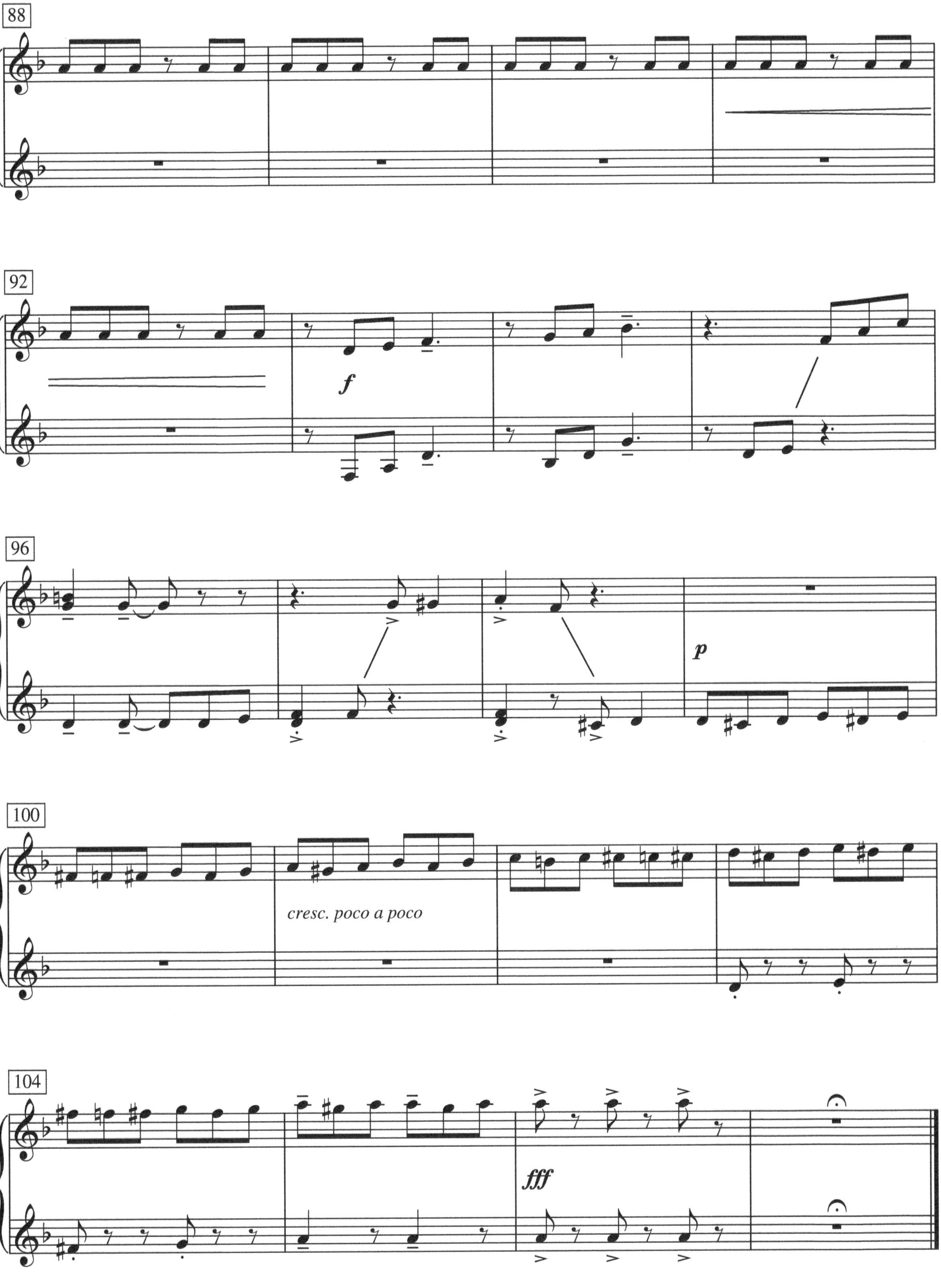

88

92

f

96

p

100

cresc. poco a poco

Piano for Two

A VARIETY OF PIANO DUETS FROM HAL LEONARD

ADELE FOR PIANO DUET

Eight of Adele's biggest hits arranged especially for intermediate piano duet! Featuring: Chasing Pavements • Hello • Make You Feel My Love • Rolling in the Deep • Set Fire to the Rain • Skyfall • Someone Like You • When We Were Young.

00172162.. $14.99

CONTEMPORARY DISNEY DUETS

8 Disney piano duets to play and perform with a friend! Includes: Almost There • He's a Pirate • I See the Light • Let It Go • Married Life • That's How You Know • Touch the Sky • We Belong Together.

00128259 .... $12.99

BILLY JOEL FOR PIANO DUET

Includes 8 of the Piano Man's greatest hits. Perfect as recital encores, or just for fun! Titles: Just the Way You Are • The Longest Time • My Life • Piano Man • She's Always a Woman • Uptown Girl • and more.

00141139 .... $14.99

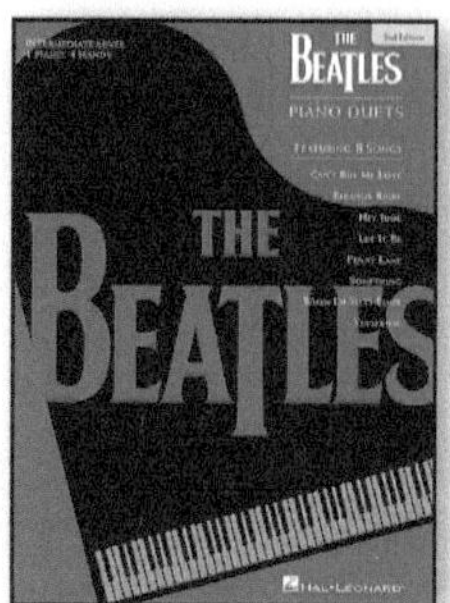

THE BEATLES PIANO DUETS – 2ND EDITION

Features 8 arrangements: Can't Buy Me Love • Eleanor Rigby • Hey Jude • Let It Be • Penny Lane • Something • When I'm Sixty-Four • Yesterday.

00290496.. $15.99

EASY CLASSICAL DUETS

7 great piano duets to perform at a recital, play-for-fun, or sightread! Titles: By the Beautiful Blue Danube (Strauss) • Eine kleine Nachtmusik (Mozart) • Sleeping Beauty Waltz (Tchaikovsky) • and more.

00145767 Book/Online Audio $10.99

RHAPSODY IN BLUE FOR PIANO DUET

George Gershwin

Arranged by Brent Edstrom

This intimate adaptation delivers access to advancing pianists and provides an exciting musical collaboration and adventure!

00125150 .... $12.99

CHART HITS FOR EASY DUET

10 great early intermediate pop duets! Play with a friend or with the online audio: All of Me • Grenade • Happy • Hello • Just Give Me a Reason • Roar • Shake It Off • Stay • Stay with Me • Thinking Out Loud.

00159796 Book/Online Audio $12.99

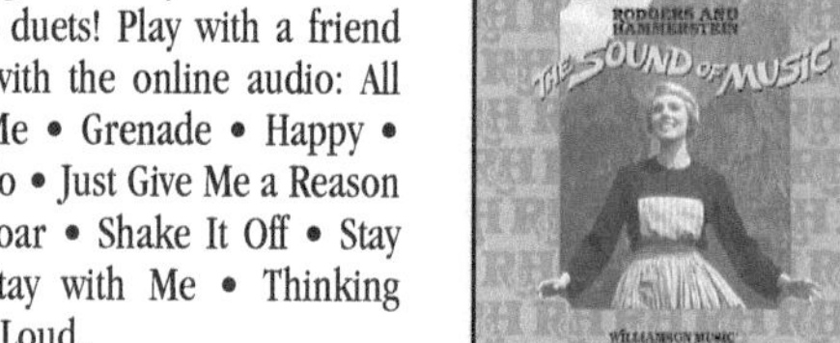

THE SOUND OF MUSIC

9 arrangements from the movie/musical, including: Do-Re-Mi • Edelweiss • Maria • My Favorite Things • So Long, Farewell • The Sound of Music • and more.

00290389.. $14.99

RIVER FLOWS IN YOU AND OTHER SONGS ARRANGED FOR PIANO DUET

10 great songs arranged for 1 piano, 4 hands, including the title song and: All of Me (Piano Guys) • Bella's Lullaby • Beyond • Chariots of Fire • Dawn • Forrest Gump - Main Title (Feather Theme) • Primavera • Somewhere in Time • Watermark.

00141055 .... $12.99

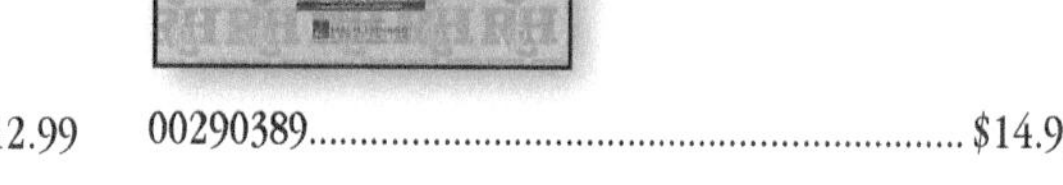

STAR WARS

8 intergalactic arrangements of *Star Wars* themes for late intermediate to early advanced piano duet, including: Across the Stars • Cantina Band • Duel of the Fates • The Imperial March (Darth Vader's Theme) • Princess Leia's Theme • Star Wars (Main Theme) • The Throne Room (And End Title) • Yoda's Theme.

00119405.. $14.99

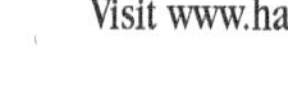

HAL LEONARD PIANO DUET PLAY-ALONG SERIES

This great series comes with audio that features separate tracks for the Primo and Secondo parts – perfect for practice and performance! Visit www.halleonard.com for a complete list of titles in the series!

COLDPLAY

Clocks • Paradise • The Scientist • A Sky Full of Stars • Speed of Sound • Trouble • Viva La Vida • Yellow.

00141054.. $14.99

FROZEN

Do You Want to Build a Snowman? • Fixer Upper • For the First Time in Forever • In Summer • Let It Go • Love Is an Open Door • Reindeer(s) Are Better Than People.

00128260.. $14.99

JAZZ STANDARDS

All the Things You Are • Bewitched • Cheek to Cheek • Don't Get Around Much Anymore • Georgia on My Mind • In the Mood • It's Only a Paper Moon • Satin Doll • The Way You Look Tonight.

00290577.. $14.99

www.halleonard.com